CREATE & TREASURE™

READY-TO-GO! BLANK BOARD BOOK

6" x 6" ACCORDION

- Acid Free
- No Prep
- Bonus Idea Brochure

READY-TO-G

Designed for everyone... croppers, journalers

How to Use Acid-Free Ready-to-Go! Blank Board Books

Use your favorite scrapbooking glues and tapes to secure items on pages. The boards give embellishments a stable surface, even brads and eyelets can go through the boards. The possibilities are endless and no preparation is needed. They are ready-to-go!

Decorate the pages with any paint, pen, pencil, inks, or crayon designed to be used on paper!

My Big Tag Book of Tags
by Terrece Siddoway

tip!

Party & Classe

Need activities for kid pa
sleepovers, showers, craft
clubs, book clubs, garden
clubs? Plan one tonight.

Teachers– use them in yo
classroom for Journals fro
the Oregon Trail, My Fam
How I Spent My Summer
Vacation, My Best Friend,
Young Author books, boo
reports, or whatever fits b
with your curriculum.

My Little Book of Quotes
by Danielle Layton

Flat pages or 3D pages look great when arrayed for display. Book by Jan Mullen

Closures

Ready-to-Go! Blank Board Book pages tend to stay open once they've been embellished. What do you do? Design with that in mind...plan the book to stand on its edge with the pages arrayed.

OR

Control your book by incorporating ribbons, ties, bows, buttons, or snaps into your design. Glue ribbon to the front and back covers and tie the book closed. Or sew a button on the front cover and tie a string through a hole in the back cover. Use the string to wrap the button.

Create your own clasp with fabric or cording. Book by Barbara Baker

6″ x 6″, Accordion, White, $6.95, 10p, blank

10 Blank pages to embellish your own Board Book treasu

ALTER, PAINT, STAMP, DRAW, JOURNAL, EMBOSS, CUT WINDOWS, EMBELLISH!

Create any one of these memorable themes

ANNIVERSARY	FRIENDS/PETS	REUNIONS
BABY BOOKS	GRADUATION	SUMMER CAMP
BIRTHDAYS	GRANDCHILDREN	SPIRITUALITY
GARDENING OR HOBBIES	HOLIDAYS	VACATIONS
FIRST DAY OF SCHOOL	PERSONAL JOURNAL	WEDDING

Front cover books embellished by:
Debra Cooper
Christina Kimmell
Judith Fender
Jan Davenport

Also Available:

3″ x 3″, 2 Pack, 1 Black, 1 White, $7.95, #20054, 8p, bl
6″ x 6″, Heart, White, $7.95, #20055, 14p, blank
6″ x 6″, Black, $6.95, #20053, 14p, blank
6″ x 6″, White, $6.95, #20041, 14p, blank
7″ x 5″, White, $6.95, #20042, 14p, blank
8″ x 8″, White, $7.95, #20052, 14p, blank
8″ x 8″, Black, $7.95, #20051, 14p, blank
5″ x 7″, Accordion, White, $6.95, #20066, 10p, blank
5″ x 3″, Tag, White, $7.95, #20070, 2 Pack, 8p, blank
7″ x 5″, Tag, White, $6.95, #20072, 14p, blank

C&T PUBLISHING

www.createandtreasure.com
800.284.1114